HRADAYASTHA

A GUIDE TO LIGHTEN YOUR HEART & HIGHER THE SOUL

RAJVI DESAI

Writer's Pocket

First published by Writer's Pocket in 2023

email: publish@writerspocket.com

cover design by Bimal Kirti

ISBN-13: 978-93-6083-026-7

www.writerspocket.com

AUTHOR'S NOTE

With God's grace, I got the chance to live through a multitude of experiences in different aspects of life which helped me evolve and become wiser human being. At one point, I realised I was utterly grateful for having people around me who supported and handled me well during the toughest of the times. Further, I realised not everyone will be as lucky as I am and hence I vouched myself to try and help as many people as I can. Keeping that purpose in mind, I started writing quotes on Instagram that were free and available to all. During the journey, I achieved multiple accolades while I was still evolving as a writer which motivated me further in continuing to write and bring smiles on the faces of people. In this path, I got the opportunity to get in touch with the Writer's Pocket publishing house with whom I had been part of the anthology named "Intoxication". They work on each and every book with depth and meaningfulness and hence I decided to work with them. The journey was not that easy as no one in my family is a writer and professionally I am a Doctor. I made mistakes but learned lessons from it and applied those while writing and made a piece of guidance for your mind, body, heart and soul.

Hope you find the book useful and meaningful in the journey of your life while you keep evolving as a person, perpetually. This book is relevant for all age groups barring readers below 15 years of age because I want to promote their thinking capacity first and then get familiarised with this book's views. Once they are mature enough they are welcomed for spiritual evolution.

With Love and Care.
Yours Rajvi Desai

This book is dedicated to everyone who taught me to love myself, either standing near or away from me.

This allowed me to understand the true meaning of love and spread it to everyone!

Just a happy and curious soul trying to make a difference and make this world a better place to live in.

Be lively. Be happy. Be yourself.

Lots of love,
Rajvi.

Dr. Rajvi Sanjay Desai

CONTENTS

ACKNOWLEDGMENTS

Special thanks to my loving and most caring parents, Mr. Sanjay Arunbhai Desai and Mrs. Tejal Sanjay Desai, and my gorgeous, intelligent, very supportive sister, Dr. Anjali Sanjay Desai for giving me the freedom to live my life on my own rules and ethics; also tolerating and motivating me at my worst.

Only and only yours,
JADU.

Grateful for the help from some kind souls:

1. Mr. Kedar Sanjay Vashi
2. Ms. Shachi Naik
3. Dr. Ajay Iyer
4. Mr. Snehal Naik
5. Dr. Kanhaiya Arora
6. Dr. Vimmy Bandaria
7. Dr. Shikha B Gurjar
8. Dr. Cyrus H Mevawala

Society has made a false impression for its own benefit that taking care and loving yourself is selfish. The word selfish has had such a negative impact on our mind for ages. But according to society's norms, if we want to live a healthy life and a life full of service then one has to be selfless. Now, I want to make it clear that if you desire to be selfless then first, you have to be selfish. So, it must be crystal clear to you all by the end of the book that both selfish and selfless states are the two sides of the same coin.

The purpose of writing this book is to take you all to an amazing journey of self-love and self-care to the final landing place of a selfless state. This book is just a helping hand for your hard times and how to live life with your own rules. I would appreciate it if you read the book and then applied it as per your priority and do what your mind agrees with rather than following it blindly. With God's grace, we have the same intelligence and mind, so let's use it in reality. Nourish your beautiful heart and pure soul more with this aid. I also want to promote lifelong learning and self-dependence with this book. I want to spread positivity, awaken curiosity and try to spread happiness with writing as much as I can.

Here we start a journey to the beyond.

Yours,
Dr. Rajvi Sanjay Desai

Chapter 1 - LOST SOUL

In the practical world, there are stages of life and states of mind due to different mindsets, struggles and experiences that fall into the definition of **lost souls**. Now that I have shared the definition of the lost soul, let me elaborate it for better understanding. Why so? Because this book is written specially for such Lost souls. Here I am trying to give a few examples for better understanding:

1) The one who is tired from life with all sorts of dramas or many failures.

2) The one who is not able to envision the future.

3) The one who has lost desire to live or is still in search of their life's purpose and discovering the path for the same.

4) The one who has recent or multiple heartbreaks, broken trusts, money loss, or rejections.

5) The one who has lost someone near or dear, met with undesirable experiences, underwent any accident following trauma, or is under any sort of guilt.

Lost souls are created because of the contribution of mental mosaic, social labels, emotional baggage, huge walls in the family and society by self, had wrong relationships, wrong financial partnerships, bound to addictions, stuck in score systems, huge or sudden family responsibilities. All this together or alone leads to negative emotions and reactions which further leads them to many troubles. Such lost souls have few peculiarities and symptoms described here.

They might cry for hours, cannot explain oneself to anyone, aloof personality, hamper relations and distance self from others or abandon near and dear ones, repetitive thoughts of running away, mind full of negative and scary thoughts, derealisation, depersonalization: feeling detached from surrounding and people around.

All these lead to a negative personality development which makes them lose the desire and excitement to live, lose the sense of reason and the inspiration to wake up. They feel stuck in the past and are unable to envision the future, unable to sustain any sort of pressure or responsibility, no determination and persistence leads to giving up on tasks undertaken, wandering from one thing to another without any purpose, unable to concentrate or stick to one statement or work for long hours. Nothing gives them pleasure or satisfaction.

These people have a part of their soul missing, they feel empty, cannot feel self in extreme cases. Even after support from people around and trained ones, no one is able to understand or help them. Here, this book's concept is made to serve them.

These kinds of 'Lost souls' are very common to find nowadays or little imprinted souls are usually around us. There was an immense necessity to describe 'lost souls' in depth because this book is written with the purpose to help and guide such lost souls. The target is to promote and help less denial and more acceptance in people who need wisdom for spiritual progress.

Chapter 2 - Discover your path and find yourself

With this state of mind and loads of doubts with insecurities, it must be very difficult for you to move ahead in life. Here, my advice to you is to follow your heart, trust your intuition and take baby steps. This is all you need to do. While progressing in the right direction, don't get confused among the numerous options available in the current times. Darling, try all shoes but choose the best fit for you.

The process of discovering your path and finding yourself is a never-ending process. The more you travel on undiscovered paths, the more you will be able to understand yourself. The more you understand yourself, the clearer your vision becomes. A clear vision will help you keep moving forward with dedication and without any deviations due to distractions. The progress will take you closer to your true self that helps you understand others too. It will let you manage your emotions and reactions so well that it will aid you to deal with social nuances. Once you have complete control of yourself then barely anything will stop you. This unstoppable version of yours still has to face hurdles but it will still face all of them with a smiling heart and peaceful soul shining brightly after any problems.

Once you find your path, have faith in yourself, do your best from your side, walk with confidence, take any necessary help and guidance, have patience and enjoy the journey.

The journey is always more beautiful and filled with memories than the destination.

Finding yourself is making you fall in love with the journey. The best part of this journey is that there is no specific destination. The more you discover yourself, the more you realise the depth within. This process must be continued lifelong.

In the self-exploration journey, discovering your path and finding yourself is one of the best steps.

So, be proud of yourself for completing this very first and important milestone.

Let's move ahead!

Chapter 3 - Go with the flow and trust the process

As it is said and observed, doubt in anything is the seed for an ambivalent mind. Life gives us many opportunities in different areas. Our job is to make the most out of them by not ignoring them. If we discuss opportunities, few are created and few are gifted. Both can end up into great outcomes if the individual gives the best.

Now, once you grab the opportunity, all I will suggest is to trust the process, trust the learnings and lessons and then trust the path. Now, with trust and no doubts, it is normal human tendency to have little fear. Here, please understand and accept the fact that only those who are trying will feel fearful.

So, first of all, appreciate yourself for having the fear in your heart and allow yourself to go with the flow. Little by little, the fear will fade away as you proceed further along, with tiny victories on the route. During the process, you will realise that it is the best gift you can give to yourself, it feels so blissful when you learn to go with the flow. In the process, you will be able to notice and grasp opportunities that you didn't even expect. Going with the flow is a little difficult because sometimes we get distracted from our own imaginations. But with a little practice of living in the very moment and with fixed attention, you may be able to progress with the flow.

In short, '*going with the flow and trusting the process*' shifts your focus to the near vision, present situation and small achievements. Because of this, the load of a huge success will end and, surprisingly, lead to big gains at the end. So, you succeed with zero anxiety in your mind.

Once you start going with the flow, many doubts will come in your mind, you might get distracted, you might fear failure but remember to just stick to the process and with some sustainability, you will see the magic.

For example, you want to follow Path A but while progressing, you figure out that Path B is better. Then just go for it. Explore things and opportunities with the flow and don't be afraid to change your path once you find a better way of doing it. Novel opportunities come in the flow, be spontaneous to grab them and make the best out of it.

Chapter 4 – Align your body

Align your body by using the following methods, I have mentioned some ideas to achieve it:

1. Increase flexibility and physical fitness:

The more physically fit you are, the more you will enjoy life without any restrictions.

The first option is Yoga and the second option is floor exercises.

In yoga, among all the different types of yoga, there are 3 main ways to achieve this to the maximum. Suryanamaskar, Hatha yoga and Pranayam kriya.

Few examples of floor exercise are squats, burpees, jumps, crunches etc among which you can choose the most suitable ones for your body type.

2. Eating healthy:

Burning calories won't be sufficient. Adapting healthy eating habits is equally important. For that, eat consciously. Try to prefer ghar ka dabba and homemade food. Switch from unhealthy options to healthy options one by one. Start your day with a healthy breakfast and you have won half the day.

3. Treat yourself and philanthropy:

To maintain a disciplined lifestyle in the longer run, I would suggest you take undisciplined breaks in between. So, for that comfort, have cheat meals a week. Try to call it comfort food, it sounds more positive that way. Apply face masks on the weekends and chill for an hour. Pamper yourself with grooming and beauty products, even sometimes with parlour treatment.

Nothing is as fulfilling and as satisfying as philanthropy is.

Yes, it is possible to gain fitness by help and care. Now, the question is how? Start from home only, help your mother with household chores. Maintain your home garden or plantation. Clean your room. Join groups and clubs that work to make the city cleaner.

I have tried to cover maximum to align the body. It is all pointless if you don't apply it in real life. So here I request to apply as much as you can. I believe in you, but you too have to have some belief in yourself.

Be healthy,
be contented and
be you! :D

Chapter 5 – Align your mind and soul

In today's world, it is most difficult and crucial to align your mind and soul. The reason behind this is that people's minds are out of control and they don't give interest or emphasis to deep things like SOUL. Here I will discuss a few options and exercises to align your mind and soul.

The first and utmost thing is MEDITATION, it clears your mind so well that it feels just like a washing machine cleaning dirt from clothes. The second option is PRANAYAM, the technique that helps you to observe and learn how to breathe correctly.

Now comes the difficult part because we all ignore mental health a lot. We feel ashamed to accept mental health issues. Here, I request you all to consult a psychotherapist and psychiatrist for uncontrollable emotions management. Take advice and help from such trained professionals.

Some suggestions to accept and promote SPIRITUALITY in day-to-day life: Start your day by reading wholesome material, make sure you have some me-time, join spiritual or positive club, listen to yogis or life coaches you can put your trust into, go for solo trips because travelling helps you explore and understand yourself better. Do philanthropy and help needy people because after all, we all are connected. The last one will give you immense pleasure and make you feel content from within.

There are plenty of other options too, like you can spend time with family and loved ones. They will fill your heart with joy and affection. You can play with kids, their innocence will touch your heart.

Finally, ending with last three suggestions:

1. Accept and appreciate small kind acts, sweet gestures and achievements.

2. Work on self-improvement rather than running in rat-race.

3. Express yourself, be yourself and worry less about other people's opinions and reactions.

Be mindful,
be contented and
be you! :D

Chapter 6 - Travel + explore + socialise = learn

I believe,

Travel is the best way to evolve!

Travel will allow you to meet more and new people. Socialization helps you learn more. Travel could be solo, duo, with friends, with family, for business or adventure or for religious purposes. Whatever the reason behind your travel may be, one thing is common in all and that is the fact that it completely switches your mindset from a comfortable routine environment to a novel and challenging environment where you get the chance to meet new people. Different and novel views from others will help to widen your vision of how you perceive things. The more you travel, explore and socialize, the more you will understand the diversity of society. This diversity gives rise to curiosity. As long as we have curiosity in our mind, it directs us by keeping doors open for new learnings.

Travel, socialize and explore = cultural exchange. These may seem awkward and difficult at the first glance but later on, attractive and full of excitement. Travel definitely needs money but you can volunteer and travel or work and travel. All I will say here is,

'Jahan chah wahan raah!'

The concept is here:

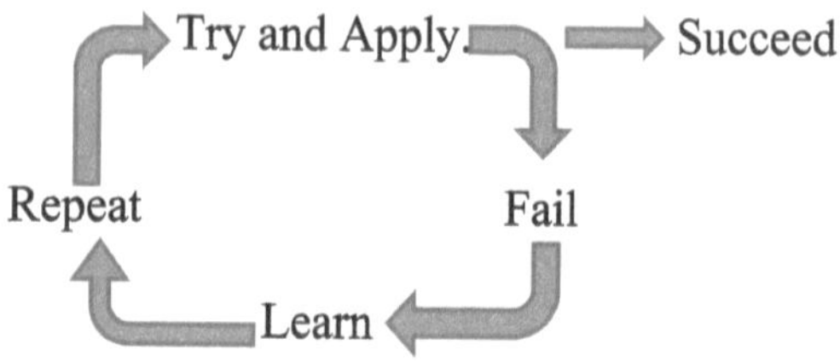

Trying new things is always fun. It can end up as 2 outcomes, either it will work out for you or you will learn from it. Keep the learnt lesson and repeat the cycle. This cycle will continue until you lose enthusiasm and curiosity. So, go for it!

When you fail your trial, you don't lose because now you are ending up with a lesson and definitely a better version of yourself than before. Failing is a big tag that no one wants and no one likes. Here, all I can say is why can't you be excited about new learnings that failure is going to offer? That way you will stay more enthusiastic, curious and evolve more. Now, you will say 'Kyu try kare hum naya, we are so much happy in this routine.' then my answer on this is,

"Roz Roz same khana kise pasand hai?

Kabhi kabhi pizza, manchurian aur cupcake bhi milna chahiye na!"

So, the moral here is, in life, trying new things is all we actually want and fear of losing doesn't let us go ahead in life.

Learn

↓

New Learnings

↓

More Knowledge

↓

New skills, learn and try new and different ways of doing the same thing.

Now, with this new vision and mindset along with a burning desire to get something done, try something new from zero and lead to magic.

Chapter 7 – Change is the only constant

"Who doesn't like comfort?"

So, once life is on autopilot mode, we start loving the comfort but change is a natural phenomenon in everything around and within us.

Keep an eye on your routine if you see any habit building up, observe it minutely before you are habituated of it. If you find it harmful for yourself or people around you, stop at the beginning only. My opinion is that rather than settling down, choose to never settle down and focus on constant change and improvement. Constant change will let you feel less of a generation gap as well.

Here I would say,

"Stagnant water ends up into foul smelling odour but running water is always clear and it finds its direction."

If you change constantly, it will let you explore all possible options available and widen the opportunity to explore them. The more easily you accept change within and around, the more blissful your life becomes.

One small thing I would like to mention,
"Be the constant and conscious change,
not mandatory and vague."

Here I have written a few lines to explain constant change with some examples:

"Printed dye fades away with time,
Once bloomed, tree loses all leaves and flowers in autumn,
Once an egg turns into chicken,
Once a brick turns into building,
Once a zygote turns into a beautiful kid,
Change is a natural phenomenon!"

Chapter 8 - Accept and cultivate your flaws

"Your flaws are too beautiful,
accept them and see the magic."

We all are different. This difference promotes diversity and diversity is our society's strength. So, according to society, common peculiarities considered are strengths and less observed peculiarities considered are flaws. But as it is said,

"Rare is unique and
unique needs to be preserved!"

All this is just a matter of how you perceive things. Some of your flaws are desired by another person. So, be grateful for it. It is said,

"How you see
is
how you perceive."

So, there is good in everything that exists, try to find it in your flaws. First, find out and then accept your flaws. Some flaws are easy to modify, and some are not. Work on the ones you can modify and see what you can do to improve them. Put some extra effort to mold it in a better way. Now, you must be wondering what about the ones that cannot be modified. Try to observe and find out the positive side to those flaws. Now, promote the positive aspect of it.

Try to modify both as much as you can and accept the rest. This way, your flaws will turn out to be your strength and you might have complete control over yourself, situation and life.

Chapter 9 - Measure the depth of your iceberg

"Only an ice scraper knows the depth of an iceberg.

Likewise, our habits, problems and emotions are very small for the world but only we know the depth behind it."

Now, the question here is how to measure or find out the depth of your iceberg:

Focus on and observe your emotions, habits, problems, complains, complications, change in behaviour.

Now, try to reach out to the very initial point exactly where it all started.

Measure the depth from the start point till now. Now, you know the exact depth of your iceberg.

Time to measure how deep, long and damaged your whole length of iceberg is!

The older the wound is, the more fibrous the scar becomes. Now, you know the start point too but the problem that arises here is that you cannot change or reverse the past. So, how do you unfold the depth?

Then I would like to remind you that you can control or change how you take or react to any incident. From here onwards, try to dissolve the iceberg with the warmth of your forgiveness and the ability to let go.

Last but not the least, don't let newer icebergs form. From now onwards, focus on how you take things and learn from your mistakes so that you don't end up with such an iceberg in life again. Try to solve issues at the origin point only rather than loading piles of it. This is the only way you may decrease load on your iceberg,

"Prevention is better than cure."

Chapter 10 - Unknot + unlearn past with redirection + replacement of memories

In life, we have different kinds of memories stored in our heart and mind, out of which some are sweet, some are bitter, and some are sour.

Once the lesson is learned then what is the need to keep and store memories, right? It's very difficult to get rid of emotionally heavy memories because the truth is that the more it combines with sorrow, the more evident it becomes. Here a doubt arises, how do we get rid of it?

Many times, the past is very dark and the more we visit it, it haunts us more deeply. Guys, no worries when we are together! To unknot and unlearn the past, we need to replace and redirect it for its reconnection to the present. The problem is quite complex but like I said, don't worry, guys. I have found easy and fun ways to get rid of it.

For which,

1. You may go to places with crazy past experiences where you cried but this time, laugh at the same place and change the narrative.

2. Go to the shady places with better and positive people.

3. Spend the same date and time doing something interesting or something that gives pleasure to you. By doing so, traumatic memories with that day will change.

4. Celebrate a day of your loss or trauma next time with your beloved people at some awesome places.

5. This one may sound kiddish and filmy but it creates wanders. Burn the memory by flushing away or turning it into ashes by destroying or harming non-living objects.

6. Stand and speak for yourself because if you are sound and content then only you can do wonders in the world.

These are some of my suggestions for how to find positive ways that work out best for you. You may apply your unique ways too!

Chapter 11 - Caution! Energy vampires everywhere!

Trust me, in life, having energy consuming vampires is the worst you can have. I do have a few!

So, the question here is, what can we do when they are around?

"Bhaag hi sakte hai aur kya?"

So, first of all, some of you might be wondering, what are energy vampires?

"There are few people (actually many, apologies here ;)) around us who are full of negative energy, talk and emotions. They don't want to come out of such a phase or allow anyone to help them come out and try to drag others within."

Or

"Some are living great lives, but they love to hamper others' peaceful and positive lives."

Keeping them away is very difficult because they are like blood-sucking leeches that stick around and continue draining your energy. I am suggesting a few ways to stay away from them:

1. Tell them directly the truth about how much they are bothering your life, ask them to work on their toxicity and come back to you only when they are healed completely.
2. Replace them with positive personalities who are full of life. You may say, that is so mean of you. Here my answer: bothering your life just to please others looks and feels uglier. Agreed or not?
3. Best way is to ignore them by keeping yourself busy with other tasks or with other people.

Simply avoid them.

If you are uniquely positive and could shift their negativity to positivity then JUST GO FOR IT!

Chapter 12 – It's your choice

The ultimate truth is,

"People are going to judge!"

Still, we all have chances and opportunities to make our choices. So, use it well and wisely.

Whether you are male or female or transgender, kid or teenager or adult or old, student or working, poor or middle class or rich, introvert or extrovert, homosexual or heterosexual or bisexual; each and every one of us is free to make a choice whether it is a small one or for a bigger cause.

To make any choice, you need to understand what gives you happiness. For that, open up with yourself and accept yourself for who you are. On the basis of your happiness, you can easily know what you want. Once you are clear in your head what you want, it won't be difficult to make a choice.

Remember one thing,

"Be aware of your surrounding and not oblivious,
we don't owe an explanation to anyone."

Making a choice is the very first step towards a long journey. Once you make a choice, the actual hurdles begin. Some will be from trespassers, and some will be from your near and dear ones. All I will say here,

"Fight for yourself
and
do not surrender!"

Still, if you decide to surrender; now it is your new choice. So now you lose the right to blame others or situations or outcomes of it. As it is said,

"Your present choices will define your future."

Rather than giving up, chase alternate options or take a hold and resume once you are ready. Giving up on something or someone is also a choice. So don't play the victim card here!

My wise and sweet words just for my lovely readers,

"Whatever choice you make, I am proud of you. Be courageous enough to make new choices and determination to live it by applying efforts. It will help you to continue it lifelong with practical reasoning!"

Chapter 13 - Live and let others live

To live means that you must be carefree of what others will think of your words, actions or decisions. From here onwards, it will be clear to others that you don't like interference by anyone. Living on your terms doesn't mean you adopt an attitude like *minding your own business*. Give a patient ear to other's opinions and suggestions but absorb as much as you like. This will lead to a completely happy state of 100% peace.

You might be thinking, come on! Is it that easy to be at peace and that also at 100%, are you kidding me? My answer to that lies in the next paragraph.

We all have been through tough times in our life and no one's rough phase is better than another person's breakdown point. In everyone's journey, their wounds hurt them with the same intensity and are equally important. Now, identify your sorrow, your defeats, your troubles and the messes of your life. Try to unknot all of them one after another. Here you might ask, 'It is so easy to tell what to do but no one tells HOW?'

Once you know the shit of your life, clean it first. Like you put on your oxygen mask first when a flight faces turbulence. Once you clean it, wear a diaper or underpants: the choice is completely yours!

Likewise, everyone has the right to live on their own terms too! The same way other people have equal strength to clean and come out of the shit they are in. Respect and trust everyone's capability and don't underestimate anyone. That is the best way to appreciate and support anyone around. You may help or give advice but only if they ask for it.

Still, if you are someone who cares like an angel (my kind of people), you may help in a hidden way. It will provide a boost to the struggling soul, liberate your soul, and may aid heal your traumas as you have helped someone who is at the same place and situation that your past self was. Finally, you adore and appreciate them coming out and now you both shine bright.

I would like to include here,

"Happiness, positivity and peace is inside all of us.
Sometimes we just need someone to help us find it!"
This is what I call, 'Live and let live!'

Chapter 14 – Conquer your psychology

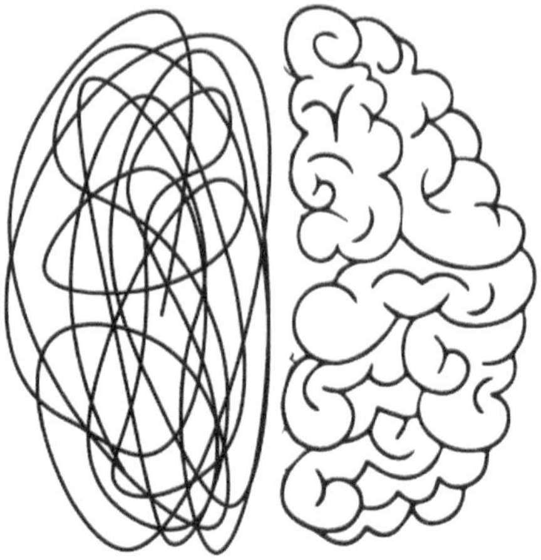

This is the most complicated topic in the journey of self-help, practically full of hassles but a very important one.

Types of psychology:

- Dominant/ submissive/ both
- Extrovert/ introvert/ both
- Direct/diplomatic/both
- Firm/wavering
- Dedicated/distracted
- Long term focusing/ short term focusing

Now, observe your personality and behaviour then try to find out your psychology type. For some people, direct command works and for some, indirect command works. You need to find out which one works for you. Once you know your psychology, you very well know how to tackle yourself in different situations.

It will eventually let you observe, understand and find out other people's psychology and let you handle all different kinds of psychologies too.

The simpler your psychology is, the easier it is to handle it. If you are luckier and hold a complex personality, you have to be very smart and handle all the aspects of your personality in different and challenging ways.

A wish from my heart is that you find ways to understand your psychology and win it over because for that, you can only find out ways to help yourself because no other person has the power to read your mind. So, manage your personality well. I am sure the journey will be long, but you will surely reach the destination.

Chapter 15 (WORLD = RAINBOW)

World is full of diverse personalities, cultures and appearance. It makes it resemble the rainbow as the rainbow has all colours. Rainbow is lovely and attractive at glance likewise the world is too beautiful and versatile. We just need an eye to see it.

Still, we have many complaining people around who are interested in pointing out problems. My answer to them is do you like to eat the same food everyday? No, right! Then why do you want to fill the world with one kind of individual when it can have a bliss of diversity like a multicuisine restaurant. So, it is always appreciated that you nurture the beautification of a rainbow-like world. Widen your vision and understand,

"CULTURE CAN BE COLLECTIVE, REGIONAL, NATIONAL OR INTERNATIONAL. CULTURE IS THE MEDIUM OF DISPLAYING SELF THOUGHTS. IT IS NATURAL TO SEE THE DIVERSITY OF CULTURE BUT IN ADDITION TO THIS DIVERSITY, LIVING TOGETHER IS A SYMBOL OF UNITY."

Chapter 16 - (CELEBRATE SMALL VICTORIES)

That's what we have been hearing from our ancestors. But we take them for granted and it costs us a ton.

Big achievement or success takes time
You may drain out or loose vision by such long time
Small achievements often happen on the way to big success.

↓

If you celebrate small victories, it will increase your confidence, fill you with some satisfaction and positivity that will make you more motivated, maintain your stamina, and push yourself towards a bigger purpose.

↓

This way if you progress it will make your journey beautiful with an easier path and less effort.

We many times underestimate the importance of small victories but we need to accept and understand it only leads to big achievements. No one ever achieved big success without long term dedication and sustainability. Starting the task itself is a big thing. Completing half or just 10-20% also means a lot because now only 90% is left, at least 10% less to achieve.

Celebrate with the ones who participated in it so your celebration doubles here. Celebrating small victories doesn't require a big bank balance. You don't need to spend a lot of money or throw a big party. Small celebrations with some close people can do wonders.

Chapter 17 - (REJUVENATE)

Recreation is mandatory if you want to be sound and work efficiently. Recreation helps to relax by providing a break and disconnecting you from responsibility. It fills you with loads of energy and enthusiasm. Now, you might question me, according to me what counts as Recreation? My answer to that is watching a movie or web series, any tour or staycation or weekend stay, spending time with nature or kids, activities like gym, dance, music or painting the heart out.

There are a bunch of people who think that they are workaholics or due to rat race and fear of falling back, they don't take a break or allot time to recreation in the schedule. Such highly ambitious people have the false impression that they safe themselves from falling back but in reality, they get exhausted, tired and have to push themselves at every single moment. Their heart is devoid of 'INSPIRATION'. Such a tired phase is the reason behind people falling back after sometime or stuck in mind with a continuous cycle of thoughts that why are they not succeeding even after giving their best.

Those who give time to self through recreation are full of energy and inspiration. Such people achieve goals easily by progressing in the right direction and are full of curiosity even after a long battle for any achievement. Provide personal space-ME TIME every day to yourself. It is not a waste of time but a habit that will fuel up or charge up your body, mind and soul.

Lastly, I would like to end with a sentence,
'BALANCED LIFE IS INCOMPLETE WITHOUT REJUVENATION.'

Chapter 18 - (SELF-TALK MATTERS)

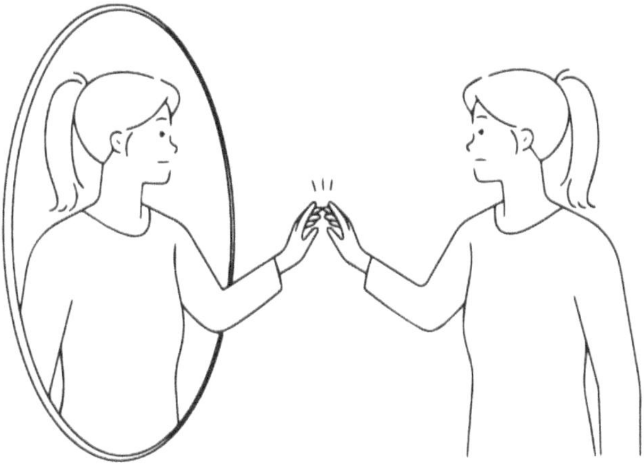

"HOW YOU TALK WITHIN MATTERS
MORE THAN
WHAT YOU SPEAK OUT LOUD."

Our thoughts build our belief and our belief directs our actions, together they affect self-confidence. The more positive your thoughts are the more positive you become. So, all I would like to mention here is that our positivity attracts more of it and lets us complete undertaken tasks with a calm mind and positive attitude.

If your self—talk is self-criticizing or self-victimizing then it will affect your self-confidence and self-esteem too badly. So, this way you won't be able to complete an undertaken task or if you do you won't be able to give your best or earn a self- satisfaction out of it. Your negative mindset never lets you feel satisfied.

So, quality 'ME TIME' is crucial as time spent with yourself will let you help focus on productive self-talk. Well then tell us what is 'ME TIME?' It is the personal space to keep an eye on the thoughts and ideas that come to your mind, updating your conscious mind of what you think that leads you to what commands you give to the mind!

Now, if you are not able to get rid of negative thoughts then journaling, meditation and even Cognitive Behaviour Therapy can be helpful too.

Chapter 19 - (MODERNISATION OF RENUNCIATION)

If you understand this concept, it can make life blissful. To understand this mandatory concept first we have to understand the meaning of 'RENUNCIATION.' Our life is going very fast to match up situational demands. Now the question arises how do we align with ourselves in this busy ongoing routine.

In ancient times, people used to go for renunciation when they felt the need to find themselves and connect with nature. Now, it is not possible for us to leave everything and go to the 'Himalayas' in search of bliss because practically if we take such a break and resume back everything around might change on a drastic level and everything we have gained so far, all materialistic things will vanish. Here modernisation of renunciation concept helps for which you have to dedicate an hour to yourself. Spend this one hour very wisely which is going to make your whole day full of life, curiosity and enthusiasm.

Some of the suggestions on how to spend an hour: Observe all your thought good or bad in a quiet room, spend time reading positive, spiritual or religious material, listen to some instrumental soothing music, Dance hard in the rain or on a song that make your soul dance, draw out your emotions on a canvas, observe miracles of the nature. If you are my kind of person, just meditate your emotions out to relax your heart, mind and soul. Still to keep it interesting just keep changing how you spend this time by trying different and all possible ways.

Chapter 20 - (EVERY ENDING IS A NEW BEGINNING)

In life we come to the point where we feel it is the end of our journey. We have done enough, achieved enough and learnt enough. These sorts of thoughts come sometimes but remember,

"On someone's death a child is born!"

It is universal law that no matter what, life must go on likewise evolution must go on throughout life.

Let me give you some examples, school ends, college begins, college ends, work begins, with work life love life blooms too which lead to beautiful children. Here nothing ends like in movies, from her life adds responsibility to raise kids right. Here also nothing ends till you are blessed with grandchildren and wrinkles on your skin until you die.

We want current circumstances to end and desire to jump on the next one by thinking that the next one will be best but all I can say is that is the worst gift you can give to yourself. So, live in the present, live your life to the fullest and enjoy.

Remember one thing always,
"EVERY ENDING IS A NEW BEGINNING."

Chapter 21 - (ENERGY BOOSTERS)

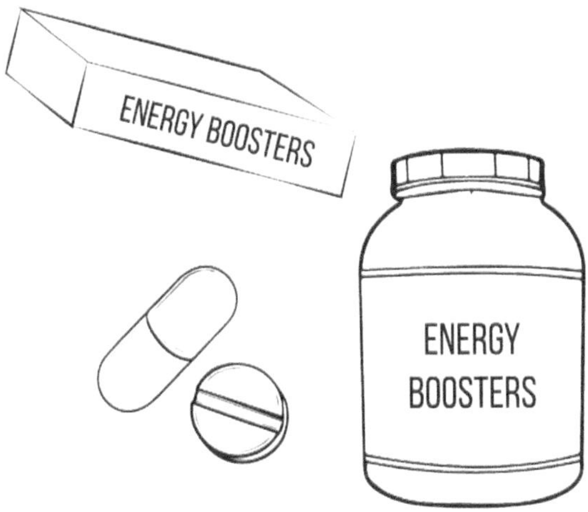

Few poems full of positivity straight from the heart written in collaboration with amazing writers who helped me to evolve as a writer. I am very grateful for their participation and allowing me to share this wonderful piece of writing with you all.

Falling Again

Falling again for somebody's unapologetic smile,
Falling again for that striking face,
Falling again for those gorgeous hairs,
Falling again for that sacred soul,
Falling again for the handsome confidence,
Falling again for that innocence,
Falling again for that translucent conversations,
Falling again for that unbreakable connections,
Falling again for the kind gestures!

-Dr.Rajvi Sanjay Desai

NOTE: Fall again and again until you find the perfect match but first fall in love with yourself because that is where everything begins! You may fall again and again while standing in front of the mirror too!🩶 Falling again and again for another person is miraculous too.

ज़िंदगी ने दिए गम कई,
पर उन्ही गमौ ने हंसना सिखाया !
ज़िंदगी ने गिराया हमें कई दफा,
पर उन्ही ठोकरों ने चलना सिखाया !
जिंदगी ने हराया हमें कई,
पर उन्ही असफलताओं ने सफल होना सिखाया !
जिंदगी ने दी ग़लत संगतें कई,
पर उन्ही ने अच्छी संगतों की किंमत सिखाई ।
जिंदगी ने बोझ डालें हम पे कई
पर उन्ही बोझों ने लोहे सा बनना सिखाया !
ए ज़िंदगी शुखारेया तेरा,
हमे इतना गहराई से ढालने के लिए,
जब हम भी अपनी किंमत समझ नहीं

शुखरिया जिंदगी
राजवी

SELF-LOVE

In today's time you have to love yourself and fight for yourself.
You have to be together!!
Nah… not at all…..
'I love you' is replaced with 'I love me.'
Is it Selfish?
No, to love others first you have to fall in love with yourself.
Love yourself, Love your choices,
Love your mind, Love your emotions,
Love your body, Love your face,
Love your loved ones,
Love your kindness and generosity,
Love your kindness and immaturity,
Love your flaws and imperfections, Love your selfishness.
Love yourself because only one of you exists in the world.

- Dr. Anjali Sanjay Desai

SPIRITUALITY

Spiritual approach or spirituality is at the core of creation.

It is fuel or energy that throbs within life. Or Shall we say life itself throbs.

Spirituality is a journey towards self-realization, liberation & freedom.

Word liberation or MOKSHA has become corrupted nowadays. So let's keep it simple, freedom.

Freedom is breaking your own boundaries or to build a system capable enough to break the barriers.

The depth of spirituality is so deep that one may lack time of the lifetime to reach the bottom of the spirits dwell, still, never be desperate or dissatisfied but feel complete satisfaction.

It is vast like space. Also, multidimensional.

As a human, one has the highest chances to jumpstart the journey towards freedom.

Meditation and philanthropy are the promising means to uplift spirituality,

Intuitions help to progress in the right direction,

Conscious actions assistance will help to manifest.

Awareness is the beginning of this journey. The process is as such analogous but can broadly be digitized in three steps.

1. Being aware of body
2. Being aware of the mind
3. Being aware of life energy.

Meditation is staying in this aware state of being.

We all are spirits going through human experiences but sadly we see it another way.

Rajvi
@viraj.creator
(Instagram handle)

POSITIVITY

Positivity is Not Just an Optimistic word.
It Is A Limelight of Darkest Hours but
we Have To analyse the thoughts of our mind!
Light and hope are present at that darkest moment too!
Positivity is a choice that we have to make every single day too!
You attract What You possess.
In Journey Of Life,
Take A Potion of Positivity,
Whenever You Feel Low, Fill It With Potion, You Carry.
That small potion will make you positive,
it will let you attract and spread more positivity.

Dhruvkumar G Gamit,
BA In English literature,
pursuing an MA in English literature.
Instagram handle: _deewrites_395

Dr. Rajvi Sanjay Desai

The Art of simplicity

In the aesthetically pleasing world, Practice the art of simplicity.
Simplicity is fascinating in itself, It doesn't need any additional embellishments.
The beauty of simplicity is innocence. The beauty of innocence is that it trumps all impediments.
The more simple you become the more integrity and purity follows.
The purer you are the more genuine and real you and your world evolve.
To master, simplicity requires zero skills but absolute efforts in today's superficial world.
Great minds of the distant past choose this path of modesty.
Modesty took them to cliffs along with honesty.
Therefore , in this aesthetically pleasing world let's discover the art of simplicity.

Dr.Rajvi Sanjay Desai
Instagram handle: @rajui.desai

Swati Suresh Iyer
Instagram handle : @Iyerwrit
BA Geography

WHAT I THOUGHT WAS DEATH

I feel like I am having a heart attack
I think my heart is going to stop beating any minute
I'm fighting for air
But there seems to be no breath left in me
I feel the dizziness in my head
I can sense the motion of every tear down my cheeks
My vision has become hazy
My hands are shaking , not under my control anymore
I can hear the faded voice of people around me saying "you are okay, just breathe" .
I am wrapped around someone's arms , but I don't get the security
At that moment I thought this is how I am saying goodbye
But after a couple of minutes , I came to know
It was just my anxiety attack.

-Shloka A. Solanki
Fountainhead school,
Surat, Gujarat.

I GREW UP

I knew I grew up when my legs reached the ground
while sitting on the couch.
When I could no longer pretend to sleep,
so I could be carried to my room
Those hours long of playing hide and seek
I think the world grew up
As iPhones replaced those plastic phones
When the Harry Potter discussions did not excite me
Or when truth and dare became too old
You know time passes quickly when
You now refer to Doraemon as 'old is gold'

- Stuti A. Solanki
Fountainhead school,
Surat, Gujarat.

MAN - ISM' IS RESTRICTIVE

Women wear suits
They are strong
Men wear nail polish
They are gay Feminism is what they say it is
Rebellions they call women
When they step forward to change society
Weak they call men
When they step back from toxic masculinity

- Stuti A. Solanki
Fountainhead school,
Surat, Gujarat.

Chapter 22 - (LIFE GUIDANCE FROM PURE HEARTS AND BEAUTIFUL SOULS)

This chapter is made up with contributions from people who are full of experience, great achievers, and sexy personalities. This chapter is added with the purpose to benefit readers to get life lessons from these lifelong learners and allow them to see the world with more than one person's perspective.

ENJOY THE LAST SHOT OF THE POSITIVITY.

Over The Years Spent In Public Service, Last Seven of Which As Deputy Municipal Commissioner, There Have Been A Few Ideas That Have Helped Me And Stayed With Me

The Real Measure Of Success Is Not The Number Of People Below You But The People With You. Invest In People And Relationships. Acknowledge And Appreciate The Role Of Other People In Your Life And Success; A Word Of Kindness Does A Lot Of Good For The Heart, Not Just The Receiver's But Also Of The Giver. It Is Only Through Others That One Can Achieve Success In Life.

The Help and Support That You Receive On Your Path to Success Leads To A Debt Of Gratitude. The Best Way To Service That Debt Is To Help Others On Their Path To Success So That Some Day They May Do The Same. The Saying "No Act Of Kindness Ever Goes Wasted" Is Just As True Today As It Was In The Past.

Dr.Ashish Naik
Deputy Municipal Commissioner,
HEALTH DEPARTMENT,
Surat Municipal Corporation.

There is a very old proverb with a very deep meaning "soft help is the last help." a person should be so confident that he can deal with his problems without depending on others, no Mini no matters what. is and everyone of us, at some point in our life come across a certain please in our life when we felt last and unable to look up with the problems it in at this line when Self help curtain into picture we can sleep into depression or cock with the situation by being confident to more on. Self help is better than any thereby route of all success and achievements in the world.

"God help those who help themselves"

It is very popular to justify the importance of self help.

Dr. Persis Homi Mevawala
(Obstetrician and Gynecologist)
Ex. Medical Office
Surat municipal Corporation

આ સુવાક્યો મારા 60 વર્ષ ની ષષ્ઠી પૂર્તિમાં બનાવેલ પુસ્તક "પંચામૃત" માંથી લીધેલા છે.

1. નિષ્ફળતા દરેકના જીવનમાં આવે છે. પણ જે માણસ નિષ્ફળતાથી ડરી જવાના બદલે નિષ્ફળતાઓને જ ડરાવી દે છે; એને

સફળતા વરમાળા પહેરાવે છે. જે માણસ હતાશા કે નિરાશાને ખંખેરી ને ઉભો થાય છે, તેને ભગવાન સાથ આપે છે. અને જેની

સાથે ભગવાન હોય, એનો હમેશા વિજય થાય છે.

2. માણસ જેવું વિચારે છે એવું એનું જીવન બને છે. જો વિચારો હકારાત્મક હશે, તો જીવન ઉન્નત બનશે; અને જો વિચારો

નકારાત્મક હશે, તો જીવન ઝેર જેવું બની જશે. આપણા જીવનની ગુણવતાને બહાર ના પરિબળો કરતા આપણું મન વધુ અસર

કરે છે.

3. જે કામ હાથ ધરવામાં આવે એ કામને માણસ પોતાની જાત સમર્પિત કરી દે, ત્યારે એ કામનું પરિણામ ઉત્કુષ્ટ આવે છે, કોઈપણ

કાર્યમાં જયારે ભગવાનને ભેળવવામાં આવે છે, ત્યારે એ કાર્ય કર્મયોગ બની જાય છે. ભગવાનને સમર્પિત થયેલું કોઈપણ કાર્ય

આપણને અને સામેવાળાને બંનેને આનંદ આપે છે.

4. જે ભગવાન પર પૂર્ણ શ્રદ્ધા રાખીને ભજન કરે છે, તેના બધા જ કામ પૂર્ણ કરવાની જવાબદારી ભગવાન ઉપાડે છે. જે અનન્ય

ભાવે પ્રભુની ઉપાસના કે પ્રા ર્થના કરે છે, તેનું અશક્ય લાગતું કામ પણ ભગવાન શક્ય કરી બતાવે છે.

5. આપણે પણ જીવનમાં કેટલાય રસ્તાઓ પાર કાંઈ વિચાર્યા વગર જ ચાલવા માંડીએ છીએ અને દિશા ઉલ્ટી હોવાના લીધે

મંઝિલથી નજીક પહોંચવાને બદલે મંઝિલથી દૂર જતા રહીએ છીએ. સમય અને શક્તિ બને બરબાદ થાય છે. અમુક પાસેથી અમુક

અપેક્ષાઓ રાખવી જ નહિ.

6. જો મનોબળ દૃઢ હોય તો દુનિયાની કોઈ તાકાત આપણને સફળ થતા રોકી શકે નહિ. ગમે તેવી મુશ્કેલીઓની વચ્ચે પણ આપણી

સાહસ યાત્રા ચાલુ રહે, તો મુકામ સુધી પંહોચે જ એમાં શંકાને કોઈ સ્થાન નથી. કોઈ કામ હાથ પર લઈએ અને કોઈ પ્રશ્નો ઉભા

થાય, ત્યારે હાર માનવા ને બદલે હિંમત રાખવી.

7. વિકલાંગતા શરીર ની નહિ, મન થી હોય છે. જે માણસ મનથી વિકલાંગ હોય એ શરીર થી ગમે તેટલો મજબૂત હોય; તો પણ કંઈ

ન કરી શકે. જે માણસ મનથી મજબૂત હોય અને દયેયથી વિચલિત કરનારા પરિબળોને ત્યાગીને પ્રચંડ પુરુષરાર્થ દવારા મંઝિલ

તરફ આગળ વધે; એને સફળ થતા કોઈ અટકાવી ન શકે.

8. જીવનમાં સમસ્યાઓ અને સંઘર્ષોનો સૂર્ય બરોબરનો તપતો હોય, છતાં તેના આકરા તાપની જેના પર અસર ન થાય અને જે ઠંડો

રહી શકે એ જ સાચો હીરો છે, જે અમૂલ્ય છે અને જે તપી જાય છે એ પથ્થર છે, જેનું કોઈ મૂલ્ય નથી. હીરા જેવા સજ્જનો

આકરા તાપમાં ઠંડા રહે છે.

9. જીવનની કોઈપણ ઘટનાને કેવી રીતે મુલવવી તે આપણા હાથ ની વાત છે. છે. જો નકારાત્મક વિચારવાની ટેવ હશે, તો એ

આપણને દુઃખોની ઊંડી ખીણ તરફ લઇ જશે અને જો હકારાત્મક વિચારવાની ટેવ હશે, તો એ સુખના શિખરો તરફ દોરી જશે.

ક્યાં જવું છે તે આપણે જ નક્કી કરવાનું છે.

10. હાથ ધરેલા કામને સફળતા પૂર્વક પૂર્ણ કરવા માટે આપણી તમામ શક્તિઓ કામે લગાડી દેવી જોઈએ. લોકો આપણા વિષે શું બોલે

છે કે શું વિચારે છે ? એનો વિચાર કરીશું તો કામ કયારેય પૂરું નહિ કરી શકીએ. આપણે લોકોનું વર્તન નહિ આપણું ધયેય જ દેખાવું

જોઈએ.

11. આપણે બધા એક જ સમસ્યા માટે ત્રણ વાર દૃખી થનારા માણસો છીએ. ભવિયષ્ય માટે સજાગ જરૂર બનીએ, પણ હજુ જે બન્યું

જ નથી, એની ચિંતા કરીને વર્તમાનને બરબાદ ન કરીએ. સતત ભૂતકાળને વાગોળવાને બદલે કરેલી ભૂલમાંથી બોધપાઠ લઈને

આગળ વધીએ.

12. આપણા ભાગ્ય વિધાતા આપણે પોતે જ છીએ. આપણે શું મેળવવા ઇચ્છિએ છીએ એનો વિચાર કરી ને જ કાર્ય કરવું જોઈએ

કારણ કે, આપણે જે કામ કરીશું, તેનું પરિણામ આપણે જ ભોગવવાનું થશે. સારા કામનું ફળ સારું હશે અને ખરાબ કામનું ફળ

ખરાબ હશે.

13. જે કાર્ય આજે જ થઇ શકે એમ હોય એવા કોઈ કાર્ય ને કાલ પર કયારેય ન ઠેલવું. કારણ કે, આવતી કાલે શું થવાનું છે, તેની

આપણને કોઈએ ને કંઈ જ ખબર નથી. આવતીકાલ પર ઠેલેલા કોઈ કામ ને કારણે જીવન ભર નો પસ્તાવો રહે એવું પણ બને.

14. આપે નક્કી કરેલા લક્ષ્યને વળગી ને ચાલતા જ રહો. દુનિયા શું કહે છે તેની પરવા છોડી ને તમારા ધયેય તરફ આગળ વધો.કામનું

ફળ મળવામાં વિલંબ થાય, તો પણ જે માણસ કામ પડતું મુકતો નથી; પરંતુ ધીરજ ધરીને કામને આગળ ધપાવ્યે જાય છે એને

સમય થતા અવશ્ય ફળ મળે છે.

લી.

જસમતભાઈ એન. વિડિયા

એ એન્ડ જે ડેવલોપર્સ, સુરત

"self love" means 'believing in yourself, the work you do, the values you uphold,the people you respect, the contribution you make to society.'

It defines your purpose of living.

"Self help" means 'helping yourself, handling situations and emotions on your own that make you self-dependent.'

Every human being has his share of success, failure, disappointment & happiness.One has to learn to take this all in a stride."

The worst also has its passing phase"

So remember what keeps us going on is hope.

It is hope that brings the ultimate resurrection.

Dr. Suresh Bhosle,Chancellor,
Krishna Institute Medical Sciences Deemed University,
Karad.

With the experience of my long psychiatry practice I learned a lot about human psychology.Out of which
I am sharing some with you all.

(1) I meet many young 25-30 year old group mothers who show up with the complaint that their kids are not listening to them. The reason behind it is sometimes mothers overexpress themselves.
For eg.
a)if a child gets injured they throw anger or anxiety to them.
b) if a child secures a good result they overemphasize and praise it a lot.
c) To make it Topper they suggest to follow rat race,competition and discipline.
This overexpression makes children hyperactive and do not listen to parents' advice or guidance.
This type of behaviour is more dangerous than deprivation of care.

(2) Each child is different so they have different software that needs different parental techniques.
a)They are followers.
They obey instruction with complete devotion.
So, they need to be instructed with information .
b) This group of children only understand when pressure is given or intimidation. So, they need to be handled with Gujarat proverb,"Soti vage cham cham vidya ave gam gam!"
c)This group of children observe and learn, they imitate or mimic. Make role models and follow them.
d)This last group of children learn from experience.
So, I request parents to provide them enough space to explore and evolve.

(3) Self-love is important but not at the cost of your loved ones. Everything in excess is dangerous.

So, self-obsessed behaviour in the name of self-love over some other person's comfort and dignity is non acceptable, it exploits your inner self.
I request Guilt prone and non expressive people not to care for others at the sake of their own self or loss.

-Dr. Mukul Choksi
Psychiatrist, Poet.

In this life of tough competition, one must never leave hopes by being

Positive- it keeps yourself happy and confident.

Discipline - it keeps you in good character.

Sincere - it keeps you in honesty of mind.

Hard work - it always pays good returns.

Thank you

Dr Manoj P. Ambali
MBBS, MS, PhD (Anatomy)
Professor, Dept. of Anatomy
University Convener Student Support and Progression , KIMSDTBU
Past University Convener Student Welfare Cell, KIMSDTBU
Member JCC Member KIMSDTBU
Past member of IQAC, KIMSDTBU
Member Academic Council, KIMSDTBU

*કોવિડ - કાળમાઁ કરવામાં ઈશ્વરે આપેલી આ ત્રણ વાતો મને ખૂબ જ ઉપયોગી થઈ છે કે જે હું તમારી સાથે Share કરું છું.:

1) જીવનમાં સારી કે ખરાબ Situation આવતી જતી રહે છે આ સમયે હાલાત ને આધીન થઈને વર્તવું સ્વીકાર્ય નથી જેમ કે સારી situation સારું વર્તન કે ખરાબ Situation ગેરવર્તન જીવનમાં નિષ્ક્રિયતા Emotional Detachment જરૂરી છે આ પાછળનું કારણ છે કે Reaction આપવા કરતા Respond કરતા શીખો જે તમારો Confidence દર્શાવે છે.

2) Try to be honest rather than following hypocrisy being something and showing opposite of it is it is not going to last long eventually people are going to find out the truth so

" જેવા છો તેવા રહો અને મજાથી જીવો "

3) જીવનમાં ફળની અપેક્ષા રાખી કામ કરવા કરતા કે કોઈ સ્વાર્થ ભાવે કામ કરવા કરતા નિસ્વાર્થ નિરપેક્ષા થી કામ કરતા શીખો લોકો જરૂરી Observe કરે તમને Appreciate કરશે અને એ રીતે એક Positive Cycle શરૂઆત કરવાના તમે નિમિત બનશો.

- Dr. Chetan Choksi
MBBS,
MEDICAL OFFICER,
SURAT MUNICIPAL CORPORATION.

Positivity is not gathered from surrounding or other people,
It is something within you,
You all need to just gather courage and curiosity to search for it,
Motivation comes and goes but
Once you find positivity, it will stick with you lifelong.
When you share it with others, it increases in amount rather than decreasing.
By sharing it with others a loop of positivity starts with contaminating all at the end in the rainbow shades of positivity.
This is the inspirational key behind my dedicated hard work and achievements.

- Dr. Rikita Jigar Patel
MBBS,
MD preventive and social medicine,
Dy. Moh. Vaccine
Surat Municipal Corporation.

IF, I hope you find fireflies to give you hope every time you feel lost in the darkness. A shooting star to guide you through every hard night. Sunflowers fill you with a light on days when negativity surrounds you. And on days when you find no light around you, I hope you remind yourself of the magic that lives in your own heart and choose to be your own glimmer of hope.

You're yet to see sunsets that will remind you of all the colours you carry within yourself. You're yet to read poems that'll make your heart skip a beat and music that'll speak to you soul. Your best days await you— days when you'll laugh so hard that it'll hurt, have coffee that'll taste like heaven, visit places that'll make you feel at home and be loved by people who'll love you for being yourself.

It's okay if life hasn't been kind to you, my friend. Trust me, you'll always end up okay, and your heart will find all the good things that it deserves.

Rithvik Singh Rathore,
Bestselling Poet,
IG: @wordsofrithvik

ઘણીવાર આપણે જગતને, જગતનાં લોકોને, બીજાઓને ચાહવામાં આપણી જાતને ચાહવાનું ભૂલી જતાં હોઈએ છીએ. જો આપણે જ આપણી જાતને નહીં ચાહિયે તો બીજા લોકો આપણને કેવી રીતે ચાહી શકે? આપણે આપણી જાતની તુલના બીજાઓ સાથે ક્યારેય કરવી નહીં કેમકે, આપણી જાતથી અણમોલ આ દુનિયામાં બીજું કશું નથી. આપણે ત્યાં એક કહેવત ખૂબ પ્રચલિત છે: आप मुऐ फिर डूब गई दुनिया । આચાર્ય રજનીશજી કહે છે કે :

पड़ोसी को प्रेम करो, उसके पहले अपने को प्रेम करना होगा। और तुम्हें तो उलटा ही समझाया गया है। तुम्हें तो कहा गया है, अपने को प्रेम करना स्वार्थ है। अपने को प्रेम करना जैसे पाप है। लेकिन जिसने स्वयं को प्रेम नहीं किया, वह दूसरे को प्रेम कर ही न पाएगा। जिसके स्वयं के जीवन में प्रेम की ज्योति न जली, उसका प्रकाश पड़ोसी तक कैसे पहुंच जाएगा? जो तुममें नहीं है, वह तुम दूसरे को न दे पाओगे।

અંગ્રેજીમાં એક સરસ વાક્ય વાંચ્યું હતું તે યાદ આવે છે: self love is not selfish ; you you cannot truly love another until you know how to love yourself.

ડૉ. દક્ષેશ ઠાકર
કુલપતિ : વનિતા વિશ્રામ વિમેન્સ યુનિવર્સિટી, સુરત

One should be self-dependent in life. One should assign time to self care, self love and self help. By doing so, you will be surprised to feel and observe the fact that once you start caring for yourself the whole universe will follow the same and start working for you.

You have to nurture yourself and relations. All these will give inner peace and happiness to your soul.

There is a thin line between being selfish and focusing on self care. I am sure this book will open up the concept more clearly.

Dr. Dinky Gajiwala Jardosh
Consultant Medical Oncologist and hematologist
Hope Cancer Clinic
Surat

"એક નઈ દુનિયા બનાયે"

હાલમાં જ વ્હોટસએપ પર એક સુંદર પોસ્ટ જોવા મળી

"પોઝીટીવ રહો, બધા રીપોર્ટ નેગેટીવ આવશે"

સેલ્ફ હેલ્પ કે સેલ્ફ કેરની દિશામાં પહેલું કામ તે પોઝીટીવીટી. હું મારી જાતને ત્યારે જ મદદ કરી શકું કે જયારે હું પોઝીટીવ હોઈશ, બાકી તો બધ્ધે કુસ્તી જ રહેવાની.

દુનિયામાં તમે જો સારૂ જોવાની જ માત્ર ટેવ પાડશો તો તમને સુખી થતાં કોઈ જ રોકી નહી શકે તેવું મારૂં અત્યંત સ્પષ્ટપણે માનવું છે અને કોકની તે બાબતેની રચના તેથી મને ખુબ જ ગમે છે.

મને તો મળી ગઈ મહેક હરેક મોસમમાં,
મેં એ જ જોયું ઉપવનમાં ફુલ કયાં કયાં છે,
ને ભરી વસંતમાં કાંટા જ જ્ઞાની તુ પામ્યો,
તે એ જ શોધયુ માળીની ભુલ કયાં કયાં છે.

હું કહું છું – ફુલ કે સુગંધ શોધવા જશો તો બગીચો આખ્ખો મળશે, શું કામ ભુલ શોધવા જવુ ? મસ્ત મજાની – જિંદગી જીવોને યાર. માનો તો બધ્ધે આનંદ જ આનંદ છે ને આનંદથી જીવવાની શરત જ છે – " પોઝીટીવ રહેવું"

હું ખુશ છું કે હું સફળ છું કે હું મસ્ત છું તેનું એકમાત્ર કારણ છે " હું પોઝીટીવ છું." મારો તો જાત અનુભવ જ કહે છે કે દુઃખ જેવું કંઈપણ હોતું જ નથી, દુઃખ છે માત્ર સ્ટેટ ઓફ માઈન્ડ. મેં તો દારૂણ ગરીબી જોઈ છે. માતા–પિતા હાઉસીંગ બોર્ડના મકાનમાં મને એક રૂમ–

રસોડામાં ઉછેરતા ને તમે નહીં માનો ત્યારે પણ તેઓ નાની અમથી કવોન્ટીટીમાં બાસમતી ભરતા ને ખાતા ને મસ્ત મજાથી રહેતા. જીવવાનો આનંદ લેતા શીખવાની વાત છે.

" શું લઈ જવાના યાર, જીવો " બસ આ પરમ મંત્ર છે – આનંદથી – પ્રેમથી જીવવાનો.

અન્ય એક એંગલથી વાત કરીએ તો કોઈકને મદદ કરીને પણ આપણે આપણી જાતને મદદ કરી શકીએ, કેમ કે આનંદ હંમેશા સેલ્ફ સેન્ટર્ડ નથી હોતો. બીજાને આનંદ આપીને પણ આનંદ પામી શકાય ને તેથી જ કોઈકે લખ્યું છે ને કે,

અંતે દુઃખ કોઈનું માપ્યુ તો શું ?

માપીને નખ જેટલું કાપ્યું તો શું ?

આપવાનું મુલ્ય છે માંગ્યા વગર કોઈએ માંગ્યું ને તે આપ્યું તો શું?

તો દુનિયાને માંગ્યા વગર ધન–સમય અપાય તેટલું આપીએ અને તે પણ માંગ્યા વગર, તો પણ તમે ને હું અંતેતો આપણી જાતને જ મદદ કરીશું.

ને બસ એમ ને એમ જ હું, તમે ને આપણે બધ્ધાય ખુશ રહીશું – આનંદ પામીશું ને જગતમાં અહીં જ સ્વર્ગ સર્જાશે.

અસ્તુ

Janak Thakorbhai Desai
B.com, LLB, D.Journ.
Ex-president- The Surat dist. Bar association
Advocate.

Matters not the destination but the journey they say.

For me, it's always about the clarity of my choices when the time is right.

I look back on my journey of life so far, I see peaks where I feel immense joy to have achieved what I wanted to pursue and a lot of depths where I've learnt important life lessons.

Since my early childhood I've been introduced to various art forms promoting Indian traditions and morals, especially hindustani classical music and dance. I feel extremely blessed being an integral part of this vibrant culture and contribute towards it with my little or no efforts.

Having awareness of our education system where a student-life ends up with a degree to fetch a job/business, I opted to explore the area of my interests at an early age.

This reflects in my unorthodox choice of career while directing two of the profound institutes in a city like Surat. Gurukulam - based on ancient Indian culture, morals, traditions and art forms. And Fifth Note - The Music School of Surat, where various music cultures are respected. I am always grateful to the almighty for providing me with these wonderful opportunities.

It's fascinating for people to know about the quality of work I put in at this age.

I could only achieve it through sheer faith in me having enlightened my self-worth. A firm voice within me in any given situation guides me through it, helping me to decide for me and my team. All it requires is a belief, a belief that I am worthy of.

A belief, if it is for a greater cause not just brings wonders to you but also to the people around you.

- Khushi Tater

To all the beautiful soul,
Love yourself!!
Live for yourself!!
Be yourself!!

Does this make sense to you?

We live in an era where self love, self worth is almost diminished.

Hardly we get to realise how deep we are drowning in this cat race. This life of ours is filled full with possibilities, positivity and peace unless we ourselves take it away.

So it's about time we check on ourselves what we are here on this earth for.

It's time to make sure that you love yourself first and absolutely do something that you love rather than dreading someone else's dream for you. It's time to be happy and content. It's time to keep faith in your timeline because that is your own destiny which no one can take away. It's time to believe in KARMA. It's time to make one good move and then cling onto it with all perseverance. Trust the process and trust yourself more than anyone else.

You are magical and different from everyone.

Always remember, there's someone somewhere who looks up to you each day and wants to be exactly where you are.

Hence, never let yourself down. God has placed you exactly where you should be so that you can bloom and celebrate yourself.

Best,
Dr.Kruti Arpit Shah(BDS)
Patissier | Chocolatier at Sweet Tooth by Kruti (Surat)

"If it doesn't make you happy, it's not worth investing your energy into it!

The ultimate goal for anything you do in life is to achieve happiness.

Be it a career you choose,
a holiday you take,
the friends you pick,
the food you eat or
the lifestyle you follow. There is absolutely no point sticking around with anything that instills negativity in you or kills your vibe."

Mansi Modi
Proprietor at The Common People's cakery.

"Not an end"

It's a new day, a new start
It's 12 again, a new dawn.

On the grave of dusk
It's the new you, the evolved you
Frightened by yesterday, excited for tomorrow .

One corner of a wit, it's not an end
It's a relay
A start to an end, a never ending jerk.

Life's dense at times
May seem like a horizon
Stiff rhythms pass
As skylines are Vista.

It's a new day, a new start
It's not the end just yet!

- Pooja Shukla

Essence : Due to the war, my career got on stake and there were months of uncertainties in my path, but as they say "until the fight" here I am, starting a new journey stronger than before!

No matter how hard we strive for perfect days, we all have good and bad days every now and then. No matter how many promises you make to yourself, you tend to do certain things you wouldn't want to do. Sometimes you just can't avoid them. This is realistic.

And, "It's Okay", if today was a bit of a failure. So, get so lost and find yourself over and over again. Every win, every loss and every mistake, will get you to the 'Place you want to be'. But every pause will take something away.

Sanjana Narang
Bachelor of Fine Arts
The Colour Story

About the author

THAT'S ME!
Dr. Rajvi Sanjay Desai
MBBS,
BA in Dance,
Pursing BA in music [Completed Visharad pratham with distinction]

I am a simple, spiritual and honest individual. I am always very curious about things around me and grateful to my parents for keeping that curiosity alive in me. I love to help others. It gives me immense happiness and Satisfaction. I write to help others evolve spiritually. My family and upbringing are behind who I am today. This book has been named "HRADAYASTHA" because it is very close to my heart and I wish it gets close to your heart too.

END WITH ONE MESSAGE,
"SMILE, IT MAKES YOU AS SEXY AS YOUR PHYSICAL APPEARANCE DO!"
HOPE THIS BOOK WILL HELP YOU TO EVOLVE MORE.
BE YOU!

Writer's Pocket

Writer's Pocket is a publication house established in 2016. We began with the aim of providing a better publishing platform for aspiring writers and budding poets.

The publishing industry in India (and around the world, to a great extent) is always something of a mystery even to the writers themselves. We are working on making publishing more accessible to everyone.

So far, we have helped over 3,000 writers turn their dreams into reality by publishing the books and continue to do so. By doing so, we also provide some of the best content by Indian writers to the readers.

www.ingramcontent.com/pod-product-compliance
Lightning Source LLC
Chambersburg PA
CBHW051359240926
51852CB00002B/68
9789360830267